Original title:
Trailing Thoughts

Copyright © 2025 Creative Arts Management OÜ
All rights reserved.

Author: Nolan Kingsley
ISBN HARDBACK: 978-1-80581-773-4
ISBN PAPERBACK: 978-1-80581-300-2
ISBN EBOOK: 978-1-80581-773-4

Shadows of Reflection

In the mirror, I see my past,
A jester's face, so much to cast.
The way I danced, how I did prance,
Now I just shuffle, but still take a chance.

Each memory a playful jest,
Tickling my mind, I must confess.
The sock I lost, where could it be?
Maybe it's off on a wild spree!

Unraveled Threads of Memory

A yarn of laughter, all so bright,
Knots of chaos twist through the night.
I knit together moments, oh so absurd,
Lost in the mix, a flying bird!

Forgotten facts float past my head,
Like a cat on a roof, it fled.
'What did I eat?' I ponder and fret,
Oh, wait! Was it lunch, or dinner? I forget!

Drifting on the Breeze of Time

Thoughts like leaves, they sway and twist,
A pet squirrel's view, how could I resist?
I chase a thought that's painted bright,
Taunting it gently, a playful flight.

Caught in the rush, I ride the gust,
A timewarp giggle, it's a must!
Moments float by on the breeze so free,
Are those my socks? Or just debris?

Fading Footprints of Yesterday

In the sand, my marks do wane,
Like a bad prank, they scratch the brain.
Each step I take, they slip away,
Laughing at me as they play.

My history's a sitcom, loud and clear,
Can't remember who's who, but oh dear!
I flip through pages, faces all blend,
Can someone remind me how this will end?

Distant Echoes

In the distance, a giggle sways,
A whisper of joy in playful ways.
Thoughts bouncing like a rubber ball,
Chasing shadows, they trip and fall.

Where did I leave my other sock?
Hiding from me, or playing rock?
My mind is a circus, full of clowns,
Juggling ideas and silly frowns.

Time tickles as it slips by,
I stop to chase a butterfly.
Why is the fridge so very loud?
Is it singing or just feeling proud?

In a world where nonsense reigns,
A trail of giggles remains.
Crammed with puzzles with no design,
I'll laugh it off—it's all divine!

Fragments of a Daydream

Caught in a web of vibrant schemes,
Puppies that play and dance in beams.
Popcorn clouds float through the sky,
While jelly beans laugh, oh my, oh my!

Socks on the ceiling and toast on the floor,
What on Earth do I even have in store?
Chasing trains made out of cheese,
Stumbling over lost memories like these.

I tripped on a thought as it ran away,
It winked and whispered, 'Come out to play!'
Marshmallow dreams that linger and sway,
In a circus of ideas, I dance all day.

A rubber chicken calls my name,
Saying life's just a silly game.
Fragments swirling in a merry whirl,
Spinning me into giggles, twirls!

The Untamed Mind

My mind's a zoo with creatures wild,
Each thought a monkey, frantically styled.
They swing from vines of whispered fears,
Tickling my brain and popping my tears.

A giraffe in glasses, oh what a sight,
Trying to read the thoughts at night.
Tigers disco dance in my dreams,
While penguins plot with silly schemes.

A parade of chaos, all in a row,
Balancing thoughts like a circus show.
What's next? A rhino in a tutu?
Imagining giants doing the hula, too!

The untamed beasts just won't behave,
They poke and prod, always misbehave.
Yet in their chaos, laughter flows,
In this mental jungle, it's where joy grows!

Echoing Footsteps

Footsteps wander down the lane,
Echoes whisper secrets, some strange and plain.
A duck wobbles, quacking with glee,
While a cat in a hat sums up my spree.

Each step leads to a curious place,
Where jellybeans roll in a lively race.
Giggles bounce off the cobblestone,
Footprints left in ice cream cones!

I tripped on laughter, oh what a sound,
As ticklish whispers twirled around.
The skip of a thought, the hop of a dream,
Life's a silly dance, or so it seems.

Echoing tidbits of joy and fun,
As I chase the shadows, one by one.
With every step, a new giggle waits,
In this romp through life, how it radiates!

Dreams on the Horizon

Napping on clouds, I lost my shoe,
Chasing rainbows where puddles grew.
They promised me gold, I found a dime,
Now I'm stuck in a funny rhyme.

Balloons in my hand, they flew so high,
Tried to reach them, guess I'll just sigh.
A circus of thoughts, where laughter rolls,
Join the parade of forgetful souls.

A cat wearing glasses strolls by a fence,
With a coat that makes no kind of sense.
I wave to a tree that waves back at me,
What's reality? I can't quite see.

So here's to dreams and whimsical schemes,
Where nothing is real, or so it seems.
With a laugh and a giggle, we dance and prance,
In this quirky world, we take a chance.

Shadows of Reflection

In the mirror, a bear gives a wink,
Off to the fridge for a late-night drink.
My reflection laughs, what a silly sight,
A dance with shadows that tickle the night.

A sock on my head, I stride with flair,
It's fashion week, but I just don't care.
With mismatched shoes, I waddle with pride,
In this funhouse of mirrors, I happily glide.

But wait! What's that? A ghost with a grin,
He's stealing my snacks; where do I begin?
I toss him a chip, and we share a laugh,
In this circus of thoughts, we spark the math.

So let's toast to the mirrors that bend and twist,
To laughter and giggles that can't be missed.
With friends made of shadows, we dance and we play,
In this land of reflection, we'll never stray.

The Path Beneath the Stars

Walking beneath a moon with a hat,
It tipped and slipped, fell right on the cat!
He gave me a look, a droll little frown,
This path is silly; I'll turn it around.

Constellations scatter like sprinkles on pie,
A comet just zoomed - oh my oh my!
With a wink and a twirl, I chase it away,
While giggles erupt like a bright milky spray.

With stardust in pockets, I try to patrol,
A crew of lost thoughts in a wobbly stroll.
They trip over wishes, and tumble, oh dear!
The night is a jester; let's drink up the cheer!

So here's to the stars, with stories they tell,
A dance on this path, oh wouldn't that swell?
We'll laugh and we'll play; it's the best kind of game,
In this cosmic circus, we'll always be same.

Fleeting Moments Captured

A fleeting moment, like a butterfly,
I chased it around, oh my, oh my!
It landed on pizza, yelled, "Take a bite!"
But it vanished too soon, like dreams in the night.

A hiccup of laughter slips through the air,
The cat laughed too, now that's quite rare.
Catch it in jars, those giggles and grins,
In this fleeting moment, let the fun begin.

A tangle of thoughts like spaghetti on plates,
I fork it around to see what awaits.
Some sauce drips down, as logic retreats,
But who needs sense when mishaps are sweet?

So here's to the laughter that bursts like a bubble,
To moments so silly, they're coated in trouble.
With joy we shall gather these snippets of light,
In this dance of existence, we'll giggle all night.

The Language of Longing

I ponder why the sock is gone,
It vanished with the dusk at dawn.
A snack in hand, I search the room,
While candy wrappers seal my doom.

A cat's aloofness speaks so clear,
Her judgment sharp, it draws me near.
With tangled thoughts and playful schemes,
I find her sleeping, chasing dreams.

The kettle's whistling, what a tease,
It tells me, "hurry!" with such ease.
But all I want is just to snack,
While socks and tea run off to pack.

So here I sit, a curious case,
With giggles lost in endless space.
In every laugh, a thought will drift,
Like socks and snacks, my mind's a gift.

Cyclones of Contemplation

I spin in circles, dizzy thoughts,
Like brainy whirlwinds, tangled knots.
A thought flies by, I chase it quick,
But trip and fall, it's like a trick!

The coffee spills, it ruins my plan,
To write the next great master plan.
Yet here I laugh; what a grand dream,
While losing track of every theme.

I catch my muse on a pogo stick,
She bounces high—oh, what a flick!
Each moment's fleeting, what a game,
While laughter rolls like wild acclaim.

So here I am, in thought's tornado,
Twisting with joy, complete with shadow.
In every laugh, I find a light,
And dance with joy in this delight.

Whispers of the Wandering Mind

A squirrel's chatter breaks my day,
I wonder what he's trying to say.
As thoughts compose a silly tune,
I giggle at a fluff-ball moon.

I roam the aisles of my own head,
Exploring realms that joyfully spread.
With every quirk and silly thought,
I find the smiles that life forgot.

A sock revolt, the fridge is bare,
The cat declares it's time for air.
Peanut butter dances on a spoon,
Like dreams that waltz beneath the moon.

With whispers soft, my mind takes flight,
Each funny thought a burst of light.
In laughter found, I've come to see,
A world that spins in glee with me.

Echoes in the Twilight

The day winds down with quirky sighs,
I glance around; what a surprise!
The shadows whisper, tales unwind,
Of lost remote and snacks defined.

A dance through thoughts, a light ballet,
The clock ticks on—it won't delay.
I see my dinner on the shelf,
It mocks me hard; my silly self.

As echoes swirl, they tickle pink,
With every jest, I start to think.
The world's a stage for thoughts to play,
With laughter bright to end the day.

So here I dwell, in twilight's tease,
With echoes dancing in the breeze.
In every chuckle, a spark of cheer,
I'll ponder socks again next year.

The Light Behind Closed Eyes

In the quiet corners of my mind,
A circus plays, oh what a find!
Balancing acts of silly dreams,
Jesters laugh, or so it seems.

A parade of socks that do not match,
Dance around, oh what a catch!
A light bulb flickers in my head,
Where do the thoughts go when I'm in bed?

Amidst the whispers of fleeting glee,
Tightrope walkers come to tea.
They spill the juice, it makes a splash,
So I conclude, my mind's a bash!

When eyelids droop and thoughts unwind,
The funniest bits are the hardest to find.
A kaleidoscope of giggles and frowns,
All in the circus of my own crowns.

Waves of Fleeting Insight

Surfing thoughts on a wild sea,
Catch a wave, then let it be.
One thought rides, then it slips,
Diving deep into comic quips.

There's a fish that tells a joke,
Flipping around like a silly bloke.
But just as laughter starts to rise,
It swims away and leaves me lies.

In the tide of fleeting ideas,
Bubbles pop with random cheers.
A jellyfish, with a grin so wide,
Teases me to come and slide!

But when I try to grab that thought,
It's gone! Oh, why are ideas fought?
The ocean's vast, the ripples call,
With each wave, I trip and fall.

In the Garden of Fragmented Ideas

In a garden where nonsense grows,
I plant the seeds of silly prose.
A sunflower with googly eyes,
Winks at clouds and giggles, oh my!

The daisies can't seem to sit quite still,
They dance around, it's quite a thrill.
A broccoli tree sways in the breeze,
Holding hands with jumping peas.

Butterflies dressed in polka dots,
Flit from thoughts, tying all in knots.
While bees buzz with a bristly cheer,
Sharing secrets only they hear.

Yet amidst this funny patch of fun,
Puns and quips unite as one.
I chuckle, looking for wisdom here,
In the garden shedding silly cheer.

Echoes of a Wandering Soul

An echo's chuckle fills the night,
A wandering soul gives quite a fright.
Stumbling over thoughts like stones,
   Whispers stretch into silly tones.

I chase my shadow, it trips and falls,
Laughter ringing through the halls.
"Excuse me, where's the exit now?"
It giggles back, "You'll figure how!"

Footsteps dance on a path so sly,
Where every thought can leap and fly.
A waltz of randomness bellows clear,
   Silly me, lost without fear.

But through the echoes, I shall roam,
Finding humor in this chaotic home.
A wandering spirit, light on my toes,
Chasing giggles where the joke flows.

Wanderlust of the Mind

I close my eyes, take a flight,
In my head, a wild delight.
Peanut butter clouds up high,
Jellyfish wave and giggle by.

A rabbit wears a sailor's cap,
Takes me on a map-less lap.
We sip lemonade on moonlit skies,
Tickling stars as they laugh and rise.

A pie fights back in a fierce duel,
With a fork as my trusty tool.
Oh, the chaos in my daydreams,
Where orange juice flows like streams.

When I land back on my bed,
A battle of socks fills my head.
In this colorful, silly spree,
Where thoughts wander and dance carefree.

Echoes in the Silence

In quiet rooms, my thoughts parade,
Invisible monsters in a charade.
They whisper jokes, they snicker and tease,
While I chuckle at my own unease.

A shadow dances on the wall,
Is that a ghost or just my pall?
He winks at me with a quirky grin,
And challenges me to join in.

Each echo bounces, tickles my brain,
Like a circus clown that's gone insane.
They pirouette in perfect sync,
While I sit back and start to think.

So here I sit, alone but cheered,
By the laughter that I've engineered.
In silence, jokes are all around,
With no one else here to confound.

Memories Unraveled

My mind's a rug, with threads askew,
Each tangle tells a tale or two.
A ninja cat with a lollipop,
Dances on a rainbow with a hop.

I reminisce about my pet rock,
It wore a hat, and it could talk.
We'd have tea with an old shoe,
Sharing secrets, just us two.

Fridge magnets play hide and seek,
As fridge light flickers, oh so meek.
My cereal sings a breakfast tune,
While I munch beneath a smiling moon.

Each unraveling thread's a cheer,
A funny tale from yesteryear.
So I'll embrace this silly spree,
For my memories have a mind of glee.

Whispers of Yesterday

In the attic, dust bunnies cheer,
In shades of gray, they disappear.
They plot a heist with a great big grin,
Stealing the memories tucked within.

Old sock puppets dance on the floor,
Cracking jokes and begging for more.
They spin tales of summer's delight,
While I chuckle at their fright.

Photographs wink from their frames,
Grandma's cat still knows our names.
Each whisper stirs the past anew,
With punchlines made for two or few.

So here in my attic full of laughs,
I gather these quirky memories' drafts.
With every giggle, I'm filled with glee,
In the whispers of yesterday, wild and free.

Woven Secrets of Distant Journeys

In a world where socks go missing,
And spoons dance without their pairs,
I ponder where the lost things go,
While dust bunnies plot their snares.

Old maps lead to nowhere fun,
While GPS just wants to play,
As I chase my thoughts in circles,
Oh where did I put that stray?

At the end of every journey,
I find my shoes, but not my keys,
The chair sings sweet lullabies,
And I laugh at all my 'please.'

So here I sit with coffee spilled,
And crumbs cradled in my lap,
I'll weave my life with giggles bright,
Each misstep a joyful hap!

Breezes from an Open Window

The wind whirls in a playful tease,
It tickles curtains, makes them dance,
While my thoughts jump in the breeze,
Looking for that second chance.

A bird chirps in a funky tune,
As I try to catch my train of thought,
But it flutters off too soon,
And my breakfast gets forgot!

Raindrops tap like tiny feet,
Trying to join a merry parade,
I ponder where the lost ones meet,
Beside the plants I never made.

So here's to laughter in the air,
With whispers tickling my keen mind,
In open windows without a care,
I find joy, whatever I find!

The Silent Whisper of a Wandering Heart

My heart roams with no fixed plan,
It whispers secrets in the night,
While my socks argue, 'Who's the man?'
In this wardrobe of endless plight.

I trip over thoughts like silly strings,
Each twist is a giggle in disguise,
Searching for lost paper wings,
As my mind tries to improvise.

On this journey of pieced-together dreams,
I find old toys and dusty books,
The echoes of laughter burst at the seams,
While my heart wears mismatched looks.

With every turn, I can't resist,
The silent chatter of quirky dreams,
I'll chase the moon, I can't desist,
As joy shines bright in the meme streams!

Sunflowers in the Mind's Eye

Sunflowers sprout in my mind's field,
With hats that wobble in the sun,
Each one a giggling secret shield,
Their dance makes thoughts feel like fun.

I pluck bright ideas like petals light,
But they often float away so free,
In a breeze that twirls with delight,
Oh what was that thought meant to be?

With bees buzzing in my ear,
As they tease my wandering brain,
I laugh at the joy they bring here,
In this garden where I feign.

So here I sing to blooms galore,
The sunflowers wave as I tease,
For in this wild open door,
I find joy and giggles with ease!

Circles of Reflection and Time

Round and round, my head goes 'whee!',
Chasing shadows of what might be.
A thought leaps out, then starts to run,
Only to trip and fall for fun.

I ponder cats in fancy hats,
Debating where to chase the rats.
My mind's a circus, wild and bold,
With clowns who juggle thoughts of gold.

A wander here, a skip over there,
Ideas bouncing in the air.
Like rubber balls that never land,
They bounce around, oh so unplanned.

In circles, we dance, the clock won't cease,
Echos of laughter that never cease.
Round we go, and what a sight!
I'll chase my thoughts into the night.

Ephemeral Waves of Perception

Waves crash in my head and swirl,
Like fish that giggle, swirl and twirl.
Thoughts race faster than a shark,
Fins flappin' wildly in the dark.

I grab a wave, then it slips by,
It seems to wink and say goodbye.
Floating thoughts on a wild ride,
Surfing chaos, what a tide!

A seagull asks, 'Is this your thought?'
I reply, 'It's one I surely caught!'
But just like sand, it slips away,
Gone with the breeze, oh what a day!

I chase the tide and hope to glean,
More goofy thoughts from the unseen.
But like the waves, they come and go,
Feels like I'm swimming in a show!

Lanterns Flickering in the Gloom

Lanterns dance, a funny sight,
Wobbling 'round like they're in flight.
They giggle softly in the night,
Winking at me with delight.

A grand parade of flickering beams,
Throwing shadows on distant dreams.
I trip o'er thoughts like candle wax,
Fumbling through the laughs and cracks.

Ghosts of ideas twirl and sway,
Making shadows of a ballet.
I try to catch one, what a joke!
But off it goes, like wispy smoke.

In the gloom, a silly brew,
Thoughts bob along like they're askew.
With lanterns bright that sway and glide,
Who needs sleep? Let's take a ride!

The Mirage of What Could Be

In the desert of what may show,
A mirage dances, to and fro.
It waves at me with a cheeky grin,
'The jokes are here! Come join in!'

Chasing dreams that hide away,
They poke their heads out just to play.
'Follow me!' a voice will cheer,
But when I look, poof! They disappear!

In this land of endless jest,
Thoughts play tricks—yes, I'm feeling blessed.
With every step, a twisty plot,
Is this the "what" or just "the not"?

So here I stand, with laughter bright,
In a mirage where jokes alight.
Join the fun of a thought's ballet,
In the haze, we'll dance away!

In the Shadow of Untold Stories

In the dark where secrets play,
A sock gets lost, it seems to stray.
With mismatched pairs all on display,
I laugh at how they got away.

A sandwich talks, it has a plan,
To spread its joy across the land.
But mustard's bold, it makes a stand,
And now the tomato's feeling bland.

The cat's conspiracy's in the air,
It plots and schemes without a care.
While I just sit in my old chair,
And wonder if it's time to share.

In shadows deep, the laughter brews,
With tales of socks and curious muse.
Each moment's changed by what we choose,
Life's wacky twists are sure to amuse.

Where the Quiet Hums

In silence there's a buzzing bee,
That claims it's smarter than the tree.
But when it lands, oh what a spree,
It learns that pollen's not for free.

The couch reveals its comfy lore,
Whispers secrets like never before.
'Come sit!' it calls, 'What's life in store?',
While chips and crumbs lie on the floor.

The toaster sings a poppy tune,
With bread so crusty, acting cartoon.
It dreams of a breakfast 'neath the moon,
Where butter dances, oh so strewn.

And in this space where quirk resides,
Each sigh and giggle curious glides.
With humming whispers, joy collides,
In quiet lands, where laughter hides.

Sketches in the Fog

In misty streets, where shadows prance,
I saw a lamp post do a dance.
It twirled around in comical chance,
While squirrels debated on romance.

A puddle forms a mirror wide,
Reflecting ducks as they slide.
With quacky jokes, they take their stride,
Embracing laughter, nothing to hide.

A foggy figure, perhaps a ghost,
Turns out to be a friendly host.
With tea and cookies, we both toast,
To silly tales, we laugh the most.

In sketches drawn with foggy flair,
The humor lingers, full of care.
A dance, a quack, a joyful pair,
In misty moments, love we share.

A Journey Beyond the Veil

Through curtains thin, the echoes peek,
A gnome escapes to play hide and seek.
His antics quirky, never bleak,
In gardens where the flowers speak.

A spaghetti strand takes a leap,
Through waters blue, its fate's not steep.
It dreams of sauce, a savory sweep,
While pasta boats on dreams so deep.

The moon wears shades, a style grand,
As night unfolds its playful hand.
With shooting stars that make their brand,
The cosmos laughs, a funny band.

So here we find a journey bright,
With laughter's spark igniting light.
In whimsical wonders taking flight,
Beyond the veil, the heart takes flight.

The Subtle Dance of Remembrance

In a hat that once held dreams,
I found a sock and two ice creams.
Memories waltz like clowns on the street,
With each step, they trip and repeat.

A dance on the tip of my mind's tongue,
Like a distant tune that bellies sung.
I tripped on a joke that never quite landed,
Now it blooms where my thoughts have been stranded.

Oh, what a spectacle, this brain of mine,
Messy like spaghetti, but oh, so divine.
With laughter entwined in each little glance,
It's only my mind that's lost in this dance.

Puzzled by paths that wander and roam,
I'm convinced my brain is searching for home.
Yet every reminder brings giggles and jest,
In the circus of thoughts, I'm still quite the guest.

Ribbons of Unwound Sentiment

I unspooled the yarn of my heartfelt glee,
And what do I find? A cat sipping tea!
Knotted in laughter, I'll wrap up my day,
With memories twirling like dancers in play.

Each ribbon I tug ties a thought to a whim,
Like a puppy that catches its tail on a whim.
In the chaos of colors, a mess I behold,
Can't find the ending, but the start's never old.

Bouncing around like a frog on a swing,
My thoughts leap and loop, what a frivolous thing!
They giggle and shout, making quite the parade,
As I follow the trail of the joy that they've laid.

So here I am, lost, it seems, in this fun,
Chasing the ribbons till the day's done.
Embracing the laughter, my worries unwind,
For sentiment's laughter is surely unkind.

Musings on the Edge of Solitude

In the corner I sit, with a cupcake in hand,
Contemplating life like a one-man band.
The spoons play the drums, the crumbs make a sound,
And solitude dances, all silly and round.

Prancing around like a bee on retreat,
I ponder my choices—oh, what a feat!
With tacos debating my lunch from last night,
And socks having meetings about what feels right.

Oh, the quiet can start a wild, silly scene,
Like a pillow fight staged by a dozen unseen.
And while I'm alone, I'll take the stage bright,
For life's just a comedy; I'll laugh till it's light.

So here in my laughter, I'll dwell just a while,
With cupcakes and whispers—come join with a smile.
For in solitude's edge, I find quite a crew,
And who says that talking to crumbs won't do?

A Cascade of Fleeting Whispers

A tiny bird chirps in the back of my brain,
While memories scatter like drops in the rain.
They giggle and flutter, then zip out of sight,
Leaving me chuckling at my odd little plight.

Each whisper a puzzle, like riddles in socks,
Dancing on tables with questionable clocks.
A parade of ideas that jump and that spin,
What started as thought turned to laughter within.

Oh, the whispers entice me to wander and chase,
Like a squirrel who's misplaced all his nuts in a race.
They tickle my mind, like a feather they tease,
In a cascade of giggles, I giggle with ease.

So if you find me lost, do not be dismayed,
It's just all the echoes that danced in the shade.
With laughter like bubbles, rising and drifting,
I'll collect all the whispers; my thoughts are a gift.

The Quiet Constellation

In the night, my socks do dance,
A playful twist, not left to chance.
They vanish quick, like my good sense,
Oh, the galaxy of nonsense!

I search for dreams beneath my bed,
Where dust bunnies lay their fluffy head.
Each funny thought, a comet's tail,
Swirling around, like a yarn that's frail.

With coffee cups that talk and laugh,
They spill their jokes on my behalf.
A constellation of my mind,
In this chaos, peace I find!

So here I sit, with glee and cheer,
Absurdity my friend, so dear.
Among the stars, I twirl and spin,
In this cosmos, let the fun begin!

Lost in the Whirlwind of Being

I'm twirling round, a dizzy bee,
Chasing thoughts, can't catch that spree!
My brain doth spin, a carousel,
In the whirling ride, I bid farewell.

A sandwich talks, asks for some spice,
I ponder 'till it rolls the dice.
Lost in moments that don't align,
Between the punchline and the divine.

Why's the cat wearing my old hat?
Dancing on tables, where's my mat?
With laughter trapped in every glance,
I join the random nonsense dance!

So here's to whimsies, bubbling bright,
In the whirlwind, I take flight.
Each silly twist, a starry fling,
In this chaos, I find my zing!

Chasing After Shadows

I chase my pen that rolls away,
It squeaks and giggles, oh what play!
Each shadow dances, makes me grin,
As I stumble, trying to win.

A ghostly friend in slippers glides,
Through my thoughts, it slyly rides.
We race through rooms with socks askew,
In this silly chase, it's me and you!

Upside down, my world's a joke,
The shadows whisper, "Hey, don't choke!"
With every twist, a belly laugh,
In the dark, we sketch a path!

So come along with shadows bright,
We'll dance till dawn, in pure delight.
In laughter's grip, we find our way,
Chasing joy, come what may!

Remnants of a Faded Smile

Once a grin, now a smirk so sly,
With daily antics that merely fly.
A sandwich wished to wear a shoe,
In the land of giggles, it just flew!

I trip on puddles of old delight,
Splashing thoughts in pure moonlight.
Each chuckle saved in jar so neat,
A treasure kept, a special treat!

The air is thick with goofy glee,
As butterflies sip on cups of tea.
With every grin that slowly fades,
An echo of laughter never trades.

But here we sit, and here we beam,
In witty warmth, we find our dream.
The remnants laugh, a little while,
In this joyful mess, I wear my smile!

Patterns in the Fog of Reverie

In the haze of my daydreams, I lost my sock,
A chicken found it, now it's off for a walk.
With patterns swirling, and colors bright,
A parade of my thoughts turned into a flight.

Clouds dressed as elephants plod on by,
While my pencil insists that it can fly.
I scribble down nonsense, but oh what a show,
Turns out my thoughts are not mine to control!

Giraffes dance cha-cha on the ceiling above,
As I ponder why my cat just won't shove.
With each giggle that bubbles and spills,
My brain plays hopscotch over all of my ills.

And just when I think I've unraveled the clue,
My coffee cup winks, "You know I'm for you."
With mirthful delight in this playful mess,
I chalk it all up to delightful distress.

Lanterns on a Starlit Path

Beneath the glow of lanterns, I wander askew,
Tripping on shadows, and the odd squeaky shoe.
The stars play hide-and-seek, dancing in place,
While the moon winks at me with an impish face.

Bubbles of laughter pop in the air,
As I bid my thoughts to 'just go somewhere!'
They bubble and bounce like a kitten with yarn,
While I spin in circles, causing some harm.

A rabbit in spectacles reads tales of the night,
While a snoring toad stops the fun with a fright.
Oh dear, how these lanterns lead me astray,
As they giggle and beckon, I just can't obey.

With each tussle and tumble, I'm trapped in this jest,
Chasing down dreams that are all but a pest.
But laughter persists with each twist of my fate,
As I follow my whims though they're slightly late.

The Riddle of Yesterday's Echo

In the echoes of laughter, yesterday hums,
Mimicking my foot taps and all of the drums.
It tickles my ears with a pun or two,
As I chase after answers that shape-shift and skew.

A parrot in pajamas squawks riddles with glee,
While I throw my own jests right back at the tree.
It giggles and flutters oh-so-lightly indeed,
While I ponder if yesterday's mix was a seed.

The clouds start to giggle, and rain drops a joke,
As laughter erupts like the silly-sound smoke.
My thoughts spin around, with no cares for their rank,
Diving headfirst into that bright ocean plank.

Guessing and giggling brings joy in the sway,
As riddles tumble, paving their own way.
With every cackle, I find I am wise,
Who knew echoes could wear such fun disguises?

Whispers of the Mind's Odyssey

On the path of my mind where the whispers reside,
I trip on confusion, but joy is my guide.
Thoughts chatter like squirrels, oh, what a delight,
As they chase one another through day and through night.

With all of their schemes, they play peekaboo here,
Flipping my logic; it's all very queer.
I stumble on laughter, found tucked in my shoe,
A giggle escapes, "Oh, what will you do?"

My thoughts play a game of the slyest charades,
As I tumble through riddles and dodge all the blades.
Each whisper composes a jovial tune,
As my mind sails with thoughts like a colorful balloon.

But as I turn corners, they giggle and hide,
Guess I'm a joke in my mind's joyful ride!
Yet, I cherish these whispers, they brighten my day,
On this odyssey of bumbles, I frolic and play.

Labyrinths of Memory

In a maze of socks, I lose my way,
Left foot in blue, right foot in gray.
The cat runs off with my thoughts, oh dear,
Is that my sandwich? Now it's a peer!

Each cupboard holds a secret or two,
The spoons are plotting a coup, it's true.
Then echoes of laughter spill from the fridge,
Why's that carrot holding a little bridge?

The clocks tick softly, whispering faint,
Time flew away, I forgot to paint.
My keys are dancing beneath the bed,
Oh look, there's a book where the cat has fled!

Forgotten games of hopscotch and fright,
Remind me of autumn and warm, sunny nights.
With each twist and turn, I smile and grin,
For life's little puzzles reflect who I've been.

Unspoken Journeys

In dreams I ride on a duck's balloon,
We quack through the clouds, to a funny tune.
The veggies wave as we fly on by,
Even the onions let out a sigh.

A garden gnome gives the best directions,
He points with style, with no corrections.
In search of snacks upon the moon's face,
Maybe a pie or a goofy embrace?

Cactus cacti join in my flight,
Dancing with flair in the twinkling night.
They tell me stories of places untold,
Of wandering trolls and mermaids bold.

With cupcakes in hand, we'll conquer the skies,
And giggles of fruit flies are no surprise.
For every twist in this laughable dance,
Is a moment worth keeping, a chance to prance.

Threads of Time

In grandma's quilt of patched-up delight,
Threads of mischief weave, far from sight.
Each stitch a story, each fray a laugh,
Of runaway pets and a clumsy gaff.

I pull on a string, out comes a shoe,
Wait, that's not mine, what's a cat to do?
It leads me to treasures from yesteryear,
Like candy wrappers and toys with cheer.

The elastic memories bounce and sway,
As I trip on the past, in a jolly way.
Time hops like a frog on a lily pad,
Reminding me of all the fun I had.

With laughter ringing through the threads so bright,
Each woven moment brings pure delight.
So here's to the fabric that binds our roam,
For in every stitch, we've found a home.

Celestial Reveries

Stars are gossiping in the night sky,
They twinkle and winkle, oh my, oh my!
A comet sneezes, oh what a mess,
Suddenly all the planets are under duress!

Jupiter juggles its moons with flair,
While Martians hide behind cosmic hair.
Saturn giggles, rings spinning wide,
As they set off on a ridiculous ride.

I find myself lost in a bubble of fun,
Hitching a ride on a twinkling bun.
The sun throws confetti, the moon joins in,
As meteor showers erase every sin.

With each cosmic laugh and planetary cheer,
The universe dances, my worries are clear.
In dreams of the cosmos, I take flight,
For in silly adventures, we find our delight.

The Dance of Elusive Ideas

A thought waltzes by, just out of reach,
Like socks in the dryer, it plays hide and seek.
With a giggle and twirl, it turns on a dime,
I chase after laughter, but it slips through my rhyme.

In a flurry of whimsy, it jigs and it jives,
Each step full of chuckles, where nonsense thrives.
A tap on my shoulder, I turn, and it's gone,
Leaving me grinning, but wondering on.

With hiccups of thought and bellyache dreams,
The dance floor of nonsense is bursting at seams.
I'll take a bow, but oh where's my line?
The dance of ideas, a comedy divine.

So here's to the jester that mocks and eludes,
With each fleeting giggle, it alters my moods.
I'll wave as it dips, in a cacophony grand,
My mind's a circus, with laughter unplanned.

Mosaic of Memory and Dreams

A patchwork of thoughts, all mismatched and bright,
Once a neat little quilt, now a flamboyant sight.
With polka dots swirling and stripes that collide,
This jumbled-up memory is my funny pride.

Sipping on moments that taste like old tea,
Each sip brings a chuckle—who knew they'd flee?
Like leftovers forgotten, they linger and play,
In a kitchen of chaos, they're here to stay.

The dreams, oh the dreams, they bumble about,
Dressed up like clowns in a colorful rout.
One day I'm a hero, the next I'm a goat,
In this zany mosaic, I'm floating afloat.

I gather the fragments, each giggle and sigh,
Sprinkle them nicely, but don't ask me why.
For laughter is glue, and reminiscence our theme,
In this quirky creation, it's more fun to dream.

Flickers of an Unfinished Tale

A story half-told, it flickers like light,
Characters dancing, but not quite in sight.
With chuckles and hiccups, they bounce in my mind,
An epic I'm writing, but oh, where's the line?

Scribbled on napkins, the plot twists and bends,
With sidesteps and bloopers, it wobbles and trends.
The villain just tripped, while the hero forgot,
What was I saying? Oh, where have they shot?

In snippets and flashes, the pages are bare,
I'll toss in a dragon, then send it to air.
A frog in a tutu, now that's quite the scene,
With laughter, I wonder, what'll they mean?

So I'll keep on writing this wondrous charade,
Each flicker a giggle, not one I'll evade.
For a tale that is unfinished is fun to behold,
With chaos and laughter, my heart has been sold.

In Search of Lost Connections

I dial up the memories, but the line's gone dead,
With static of chuckles buzzing in my head.
A voice from the past says it's been on the fritz,
Oh dear, what a mess, just a myriad of bits.

I wander through echoes of laughter and cheer,
Searching for signals that flicker and veer.
My phone's just a relic; it's lost all its grace,
In this comedy show, I've lost my own face.

Each link is a riddle, a puzzle in jest,
With connections like noodles all tangled and pressed.
I tug, and I pull, but they simply won't budge,
This network of nonsense—I just want to grudge.

Yet here in the chaos, there's joy to unwrap,
For every lost connection can turn into rap.
I'll start a new dance with the quirks and the quirks,
In search of lost laughter, my heart really perks.

Reflections in the Quiet

In silence I ponder, what was that joke?
Did I really just ask, if my cat likes to smoke?
When the mind goes a-wandering, it takes quite the trip,
Like a squirrel on a skateboard, with a fancy flip.

Thoughts tumble like laundry, all mixed in a heap,
I can't find my car keys, my brain must be asleep.
Coffee stains on my shirt, a badge of my plight,
Why does my left shoe feel heavy but right?

I muse over snacks, a true epicure,
Last night's pizza was love, that I must ensure.
But why did I leave half, all cold in a box?
My appetite's clever, my brain has the flocks.

As laughter erupts, from my own little mind,
A poke at the humor, it's all of a kind.
Life's but a circus, the show must go on,
So here's to my thoughts, let's sing them a song!

A Tapestry of Mindscapes

My mind's like a bird, flapping everywhere,
It landed on nonsense, forgot how to care.
A tapestry woven, in colors awry,
With glittery patches of chicken pie.

I pondered my purpose while lost in a dream,
Did I set the timer or just caught the stream?
Imagined a world where socks all have pairs,
And unicorns dance, with no worldly cares.

Thoughts flit like butterflies, what are they seeking?
Should I chase down the snacks, or keep on tweaking?
Oh look, there's my old friend, the toaster of fate,
Enticing my cravings, oh isn't it great?

In this endless musing, I chuckle and grin,
For life's a jigsaw, let the fun begin.
A tapestry stretched, by the quirks of our minds,
Each stitch tells a story, where laughter unwinds.

Where Thoughts Roam Free

Thoughts drift like balloons on a bright summer day,
I reached for a snack but got lost on the way.
Do thoughts have a map, or just follow the breeze?
Maybe they're squirrels, bouncing high in the trees.

In the land of the silly, I'm king of the jest,
Did I wear mismatched socks as my daily quest?
When pondering life, it's the little things bright,
Like penguins in tuxedos, all ready to fight.

My brain does a jig, every few words I hear,
Making shapes of ideas, while chugging my beer.
Spinning tales of chaos while sipping on tea,
Oh where will they glide off, my thoughts, wild and free?

As they soar to the heavens, I sit here and smile,
Embracing the nonsense, I'll stay for a while.
The thoughts swirl around, like confetti in air,
So here's to the laughter, I'm happy to share!

Veil of Nostalgia

In the attic of memories, dust bunnies play,
Did I really wear that? Oh my, what a day!
With each curious trinket, a chuckle appears,
Like old photo albums that bring back the cheers.

Thoughts tangled like hair, from a wild little run,
Life's quirks are hilarious, all meant to be fun.
I trip over time, in this land of the past,
Nibbling on moments, a taste that won't last.

So here's to the times, we forgot what we wore,
Like helmets for riding, to old candy stores.
Sneakers with holes, smiles wide as the sun,
Making goofy faces, for laughs — we have won!

With a wink and a nod, I embrace all that's gone,
For laughter's the vessel that carries us on.
In the veil of nostalgia, I jump with great glee,
Let's toast to our days, and the memories we see!

The Space Between Moments

In the seconds that tick just too slow,
I ponder on why we all say, "Hello!"
As if each greeting might change the whole day,
But we just laugh and then walk the same way.

I trip on my thoughts like a shoelace untied,
Wondering where my ice cream did hide.
It melts on my fingers, a sticky delight,
Yet still I just scoop it and take another bite.

The pause in a joke is a curious art,
Like planting a seed in a warm, sunny spot.
I wait for your laughter to bloom and to start,
Then realize, oh wait, that was just a bad plot.

But still in the gaps, there's a spark of the fun,
We dance in the spaces, unified as one.
With quirks and with chuckles, we giggle and run,
In the space between moments, laughter's begun.

Dandelion Seeds of Introspection

I blow on the dandelions, puffing with zest,
Hoping for wishes to land as a jest.
They float on the breezes, like thoughts that I chase,
While I'm stuck in this place with a grin on my face.

A butterfly lands on my nose with a flair,
I sneeze, then it flies like it just doesn't care.
Introspective today? Or just silly and bright?
Both options feel great when you're high as a kite.

I wonder what happens when I take a break,
Do the thoughts wear capes or just wander and shake?
Do the seeds keep on drifting in glorious flight,
Finding strange lands where they twirl through the night?

So here I just sit with my dandelion dreams,
Each whim a balloon bursting at the seams.
I chase down the laughter with laughter that beams,
For life's such a puzzle, or so it seems!

A Tapestry of Wandering Memories

I stitch up my memories, colorful threads,
One's of a cat wearing socks on its heads.
A patch full of pie fights and laughter galore,
Oh, what a fine tale we could always explore!

There's a moment of silence, a glitch in my thought,
Did I really just ask if I think I forgot?
With wisdom like noodles, I twirl and I spin,
In a tapestry woven from chaos within.

I hang up my moments, a gallery bright,
With paintings of mishaps, a comical sight.
I chuckle at times when I once lost my shoe,
And danced through the rain like a crazy old fool!

So here is my tale, all jumbled and fun,
A tapestry blasting with joy on the run.
In slices of laughter, I mix in the sun,
For wandering memories are never quite done.

Haunting Melodies of What Was

I hear echoes of laughter that stirs in the gloom,
Like ghosts who refuse to depart from the room.
Each melody whispers of mischief and cheer,
A serenade played by the friends we hold dear.

I dance with the shadows, a quick-footed polka,
While dodging the chime of a long-lost old yoke-a!
What was once high drama is now just a jest,
As I chuckle at life's playful little quest.

The songs of the past tickle my mind,
While prancing through memories, so unconfined.
A waltz through the years that feels quirky and bright,
Like a cat with a hat in the pale moonlight.

So let's raise a glass to the ghosts and their tunes,
To laughter and chaos that dance with the moons.
For hauntingly funny are the moments we share,
In melodies drifting on wonderfully rare air.

The Road Less Remembered

I took a trip down memory lane,
But the map had a coffee stain.
Each turn led to a funny face,
Lost in a rather silly place.

I met my past, it wore a hat,
And spoke like a quirky little brat.
It pointed east, then west, then back,
Whispering secrets I lost in the crack.

There's a zebra crossing for my old shoe,
And every step smelled like barbecue.
A sign said, 'Dance, don't forget to sing!'
I better call my mom, she'll have a fling!

Oh, how I stumbled through that day,
With my shoes untied and thoughts at play.
Each moment was a wobbling charade,
On the road where my brain got delayed.

Glimpses of Forgotten Echoes

I heard a laugh from days of yore,
It slipped through the cracks and out the door.
Echoes bounced like rubber balls,
Hitting memories on silly walls.

I chased an echo, it giggled and swirled,
In a world where silly thoughts twirled.
Forgotten jokes began to unroll,
Like misfit socks that lost their soul.

A phantom taught me how to jest,
With punchlines that never took a rest.
We dined on humor, sipped on glee,
Then slipped on laughter—my, what glee!

In the nook of yesterday's scheme,
I found a treasure that would beam.
It winked and said, 'Take me home,
I'll make you laugh while you roam!'

Between the Silence and the Sound

There's a whisper lost in the breeze,
Betwixt the silence and the sneeze.
A joke hides behind the quiet wall,
Waiting for someone to hear its call.

I searched for laughter in a quiet room,
But tripped on a sock and met my doom!
A tickle echoed from a dusty chair,
I laughed so hard, I filled the air.

Between the tick and the tock,
A giggle nestled like a ticking clock.
I caught it fast, like catching flies,
And teased it with some silly lies.

Now silence dances with a tune,
As laughter howls like a cheerful moon.
Between the beats where thoughts collide,
I found the joy that I can't hide!

Chasing the Ghosts of Thought

I chased a ghost down a winding lane,
It laughed and turned, feeding my brain.
Every idea was a funny sight,
Floating like bubbles in broad daylight.

It danced on the tips of silly dreams,
Sipping on ice cream in sunlit beams.
'Catch me if you can!' the phantom cried,
And off it fluttered like a kite with pride.

I pulled a shoelace, stumbled a bit,
Tried to keep pace with that cheeky wit.
Thoughts darted left, then flopped to the right,
In a merry chase that felt just right.

As we twirled 'neath a sky so blue,
The ghost taught me how to laugh anew.
Now I haunt my own mind's fair ground,
With echoes of happiness all around!

Tides of Uncertainty

In my head, ideas roll,
Like waves on a beach, they stroll.
One moment bright, a sunny day,
The next, they're lost, just fade away.

A thought like a fish, it slips and slides,
Chasing it feels like a wild ride.
Splashing around in this thought-filled sea,
I wonder if this fish is really me.

A bucket of dreams, I try to catch,
Each thought escapes, I lose the match.
With each tide, I laugh and sigh,
Where do they go? Oh, me oh my!

Waves crash down on the shores of fate,
I build my castles but they can't wait.
A beachfront of humor, a comical scene,
As thoughts run amok, like a clown in a dream.

The Path of Swaying Sentiments

On a road of feels, I take a stroll,
I trip on laughter, then lose control.
A tear-soaked giggle decides to dance,
It winks at my heart, a chance romance.

Thoughts wobble like jelly, oh what a sight,
Some flip like pancakes, they take flight.
A walk on this path, a jolly mishap,
With each switch in mood, I pull a funny cap.

Bump into joy, knock down some gloom,
A tumble of thoughts, they rush like a broom.
In this merry chaos, I hold tight my grin,
For each twist of fate could lead to a win.

Through puddles of giggles, I carefully tread,
A circus of feelings inside my head.
With a hop and a skip, I dance down this lane,
Who knew swaying sentiments could be so insane?

Traversing the Landscape of the Mind

In my mind's garden, a thought grows tall,
But wait, there's a bunny! Off it does sprawl.
It hops over dreams and through tangled schemes,
While I'm stuck here chasing my own wild dreams.

Mountains of worries loom over my head,
Each peak holds a thought that can't be fed.
Climbing high just to see the view,
Oh wait! Is that a clown? Just passing through?

The rivers of ponder flow steady and bright,
But sometimes they bubble and bring thoughts to fight.
A splash of confusion, a sprinkle of cheer,
As I laugh at the chaos that's swirling near.

Oceans of whims crash with comical force,
A boat full of chuckles sets a lively course.
In this silly venture, no need for a map,
Just ride on the waves, in a giggly trap!

Reflections on the Surface of Still Water

I gaze at the pond, oh, such a great place,
Reflections of thoughts make funny faces.
A duck quacks a joke, I can't help but grin,
While a frog jumps in, saying, "Let's begin!"

Ripples of laughter dance on the shore,
Each wave brings a giggle, who could ask for more?
In this tranquil surface, chaos is found,
Jokes echo softly, as joy spins around.

Clouds above play hide and seek with the sun,
Each shadow a punchline, oh, isn't this fun?
The water reflects, yet it dances with glee,
As thoughts take a plunge, wild and free.

I skip a stone; it bounces just right,
Each hop is a chuckle, pure delight.
So here by the water, I clear out my head,
With laughter as my compass, I'll happily tread.

The Elusive Nature of Memory

I searched my mind for a snack,
Yet all I found was a faded plaque.
It promised me a trip to the past,
But the path was lost; it disappeared fast.

In the pantry of thought, a can rolls away,
The label's gone; can't recall what it may.
I laugh as I ponder what once was bold,
Now just a few crumbs, memories cold.

A whisper of laughter on a sunlit day,
But where it went off, I just can't say.
Like socks in the dryer, they vanish, I swear,
Left wondering if they had a secret affair.

So here's to the memories that tease and delight,
More like balloons that float out of sight.
I'll chase down a thought, like a cat with a feather,
But catch it I won't, not now, not ever!

Through the Looking Glass of Time

I peek through the glass, a time traveler's glee,
But the view is so blurry; is that really me?
A reflection of chaos, a whimsical dance,
I ponder my journey, give fate a chance.

Tick-tock goes the clock, what is that sound?
Oh wait, it's my neighbor; he's spinning around.
He's stuck in a moment, a memory's grip,
As I chuckle and watch, sipping coffee, a sip.

I laugh at the recollections that jolt,
Each a peculiar twist in the time-vault.
A party of seconds throwing confetti on me,
While the future and past just sip on their tea.

In the mirror, I see a mishmash of fun,
Like jelly and jam mixed under the sun.
So I wave at my self from the years gone away,
And tumble through time in a zany ballet.

Fishermen of Thoughts in a Sea of Dreams

We cast our nets where the thoughts like to swim,
Hoping for treasures, on a whim.
But the fish are clever, they wriggle and squirm,
Leaving us chuckling at our own mind's term.

A big one darts and eludes our grasp,
While we tell tall tales, and awkwardly gasp.
Each catch is a giggle, a snicker, a sigh,
As we haul in the nonsense, oh my, oh my!

Floating ideas bob like corks in the brine,
Some bizarre, others oddly divine.
We feast on the visions, so sweet and bizarre,
Like candy floss dreams spun from a shooting star.

Each reel in a laughter, a story to tell,
Of efforts and blunders, we know them so well.
In this surreal fishing, we're all quite the team,
Casting wide with our nets in a sea full of dream.

The Breath of the Unfinished Journey

Off I go with a map that's upside down,
Compass spinning wildly, a real circus clown.
I skip through the trails, each step a new quest,
Stumbling on questions, my mind is a jest.

The path is a riddle, full of twists and turns,
And every lost thought is a spark that burns.
With a chuckle I trip on a pebble of doubt,
Yet giggle it off, what's a journey without?

The suitcase is heavy, it's filled with my dreams,
Yet half of it's filled with the silliest beams.
Like socks in a dryer, my plans get so wild,
I toss them all out, like a mischievous child.

So onward I wander, with hope in my shoe,
Chasing the sun, and the clouds that are blue.
This journey unfinished may lead to the best,
With laughter and whimsy, I'm truly blessed.

Paths Untrodden in the Mind's Forest

In the woods where lost socks roam,
A squirrel debates which nut is home.
Birds gossip in an acorn hat,
While trees laugh at a wandering cat.

A path appears, but who can tell?
If it leads to heaven or just a shell.
A bunny hops, its nose a twitch,
Stumbles upon a lopsided pitch.

The wind plays tricks, it tells sly jokes,
While each little branch hosts a party of folks.
Wandering away, my train of thought,
Is racing behind—a funny knot.

Down buried trails where dreams collide,
A bear thinks it's Wednesday—what a wild ride!
Rambling whispers ride the breeze,
Of old socks debating life with ease.

Whispers on the Edge of the World

At the edge of the world where the sea fits right,
Ninjas of seaweed plan the fort's next fight.
Seagulls trade secrets with winks and squeaks,
While crabs recite poems about their peaks.

A lighthouse blinks, a Morse code fable,
As sardines plot to steal a table.
Fish toss coins for a wish or two,
While lobsters laugh at a shrimp's debut.

Whispers dance on the wind so light,
Leading my thoughts into the night.
Sunsets giggle as they paint the sky,
While waves clap hands, oh me, oh my!

At corners where shadows twist and turn,
The world spins secrets, let them burn.
Each stray thought drifts on salty breeze,
As the ocean hums beneath the trees.

Spirals of Uncertain Memories

In spirals where old chairs sit and sigh,
A cat recalls how to leap and fly.
Remembering past lives, with laughter abound,
As socks misplace their purpose—oh, profound!

Twirling in circles like a dizzy whiz,
What was that fact? Oh, what was it?
Memories graze like cows in a field,
Munching on thoughts that refuse to yield.

A garden of giggles grows round and round,
Where weeds wear hats, they're quite renowned.
Each nugget of thought a pom-pom sprout,
Chasing the echoes that flounce about.

Through the junkyard of pasts that gleam and blush,
Where even old doors whisper, 'Don't rush!'
Each turn of phrase in this mental dance,
Keeps slipping away, but I'll take the chance.

The Weight of Unspoken Words

In a meeting, oh so serious,
My mind drifts, oh so delirious.
Thoughts of lunch dance in my head,
Forget the agenda, let's just be fed.

The boss speaks of profits and gloom,
While I map chocolate shops in the room.
Words hang heavy, like clouds of gray,
I scribble doodles, 'What's for lunch today?'

My brain's a circus, thoughts taking flight,
Juggling punchlines, oh what a sight!
With every pause, I hear the sound,
Of giggles and snickers, laughter abound.

The clock hands move slow, as if in a trance,
I plot my escape, oh what a chance!
One snicker, one wink, and I'll surely burst,
In this sea of silence, my humor's dispersed.

Footprints on a Seashore of Time

Walking by the shore, my mind takes a stroll,
Seagulls are squawking, they'll take a toll.
A sandcastle here, a bucket lost there,
My thoughts wander off without a care.

With every wave, the past creeps near,
Was that really me in that old gear?
A boogie board and a really bad tan,
If only back then, I had a better plan!

Footprints washed away, it's such a sight,
But I'll keep laughing at my fashion blight.
A beach ball's rolling into my face,
Oh memories, you're such a funny place!

The tide brings back moments, some bittersweet,
Of ice cream melt and sandy, sticky feet.
Each grain a chuckle from a sunny day,
As I chase my thoughts, but they run away!

Vanilla Skies of Nostalgia

Under vanilla skies, my youth calls aloud,
The ice cream truck, oh what a crowd!
Chasing flavors, forgotten dreams,
Wasting summers in wild, sugary schemes.

Old friends retell our shenanigans bright,
Like that time we wore socks that didn't quite match right.

Laughter fills the air, a sweet, funny tune,
As we launched water balloons, oh what a boon!

The memories bounce like kids on a trampoline,
Full of nonsense, laughter, and candy machine.
With every giggle, I reminisce and sigh,
Oh to be young, 'til strawberry pie.

But here I stand with a smile so wide,
With goofy thoughts that I cannot hide.
Life's a tasty swirl, a joyful surprise,
And who knew nostalgia could come with fries?

The Palette of Unconscious Longings

In a room full of colors, I ponder the hue,
What shade am I feeling, oh what a view?
A splash of red for the pizza I crave,
With hints of blue in a daydream wave.

Painting my heart with strokes so absurd,
A canvas of craving, without a word.
The palette's messy, it hardly stays neat,
As I mix my desires, my thoughts take a seat.

With every twist, the colors collide,
Green for the salad, my taste buds' pride.
A dash of giggles, a swirl of delight,
Let's paint this craving with humor tonight!

Yet here I stand with my brush in a spin,
Realizing my longing is just for a win.
A masterpiece hidden in laughter and cake,
Oh the joy of a whim, just for goodness' sake!

Driftwood Thoughts on an Endless Sea

As I float on waves of whimsy,
A seagull steals my snack, oh flimsy!
Mind drifts like wood, on currents wide,
With jellyfish dreams, I curl and glide.

Each thought a fish, that flips and sways,
Beneath the sun's warm, golden rays.
I chase my mind like bubblegum,
Bouncing here and there, so very glum.

Tides bring laughter, tides bring cheer,
But why does the ocean smell like beer?
Sailing on giggles, I lose the flow,
Caught in a whirlpool of cheese and dough.

Oh, the tide pulls me, I must confess,
My thoughts like driftwood, a comedic mess.
In laughter, I float, in silliness, thrive,
Just an absurd pine who's happy to dive.

The Uncharted Map of Mind

With a compass of chaos I wander round,
In the maze of thoughts where silly is found.
Maps drawn in crayon, lead to lost space,
An x marks the spot for my sock's hiding place.

I traced the lines but crossed a few,
Where was I going? No clue, boo-hoo!
A treasure chest? Oh wait, it's a shoe,
Tangled in riddles, like spaghetti too!

The north star's a gumdrop, bright and spry,
Maps that I make tend to go awry.
Each turn I take, I take with a grin,
To find out where I was, is it just a whim?

Yet every misstep leads to a laugh,
A misprinted map? A comedic gaffe!
Adventuring through this silly maze,
Finding joy in the quirks, in mind's wacky ways.

Fleeting Glimpses of a Dreamscape

In dreamscapes where pancakes float like clouds,
I ride on a turtle who totally crowds.
Thoughts are like fireflies, buzzing in flight,
Tickling my brain, oh what a delight!

Through candy fields where fruitcakes rain,
Silly visions like clowns on a train.
A carousel spins, but it's just me,
Wearing a hat made of brie and a pea.

Mice in tuxedos are part of the scene,
Playing chess with a frog, oh so keen!
Whimsical realms intertwine and bend,
Each laugh a journey, around every bend.

Yet morning light breaks this fun-filled spree,
And I awaken to reality's decree.
But the echoes of giggles, I'd never trade,
For a world of dreams, where I'm never afraid.

Sighs of Pondered Existence

Oh, the sighs of thinkers, with coffee in hand,
Wondering if life's just a band on demand.
From pondering life's meaning to snack breaks at best,
Philosophy's like pizza—it's all in the quest!

When thoughts wander off, like sheep on the roam,
I chase them with humor, bringing them home.
Laughing at seriousness, oh what a chore,
Life's best when silly walks through the door.

Existence, it seems, is a comedy play,
With pratfalls and punchlines in disarray.
Yet in every moment, I find the laugh,
In the throes of deep thought, and a cheeky half.

So cheers to the ponderers, the sneezers of thought,
In the absurdity of living, such wonders are caught.
With each little sigh, I reshape the view,
Existence is funny, I hope you think so too!

The Currents of Unspoken Dreams

Bubbles rise in a fizzy drink,
Unseen laughter floats and winks.
Whispers chase on giddy tides,
A giggle rides and never hides.

Thoughts like fish in squishy bowls,
Wobble and flip like untrained shoals.
They dart away, then swim back near,
Tickling memory, defying fear.

Clouds parade on a summer's day,
Mimicking sheep in a playful way.
Suddenly one escapes the flock,
To join a party on the clock.

In the world of jumbled schemes,
Cacophonies create sweet dreams.
Unraveling giggles, silly scenes,
In currents blurred by laughter's means.

Lost in the Labyrinth of Ideas

Round and round in a wacky maze,
Thoughts like squirrels in a nutty craze.
Chasing shadows, one twist, then a turn,
In this puzzle, I gladly churn.

Tickling mazes with a whimsical spark,
Every corner hides a giggling lark.
In a spiral dance, I take each stride,
Finding carrot trails, where jokes collide.

Crumbling puzzles, layers unfold,
Each thought scribbled strikes like gold.
A map made of candy, leading me on,
In the maze's heart, I've finally won!

With every detour, I burst into glee,
Lost in laughter; oh, let it be!
Jumbled turns bring jovial keeps,
In a labyrinth where mischief leaps.

Fleeting Moments, Endless Journeys

Capturing giggles in jars of the past,
Moments like bubbles, they never last.
A tickle of time, and then they burst,
Riding on whims, forever thirst.

With sandwiches flying on breezy days,
Each laugh igniting a new array.
Chasing frolics down the sunny lanes,
As joy bounces like runaway trains.

Twirls of folly in a fleeting dance,
Each step uncertain, a playful chance.
Every giggle a passport to roam,
In the land of joy, I find my home.

Fragments of laughter, a kaleidoscope view,
Past moments echo, both old and new.
Adventures grow shorter as giggles grow bold,
In my memory's scrapbook, life's tales are told.

Fragments of a Tattered Mind

Jigsaw pieces from a chuckling past,
Memories flutter, too wild to cast.
Fleeting visions of donuts and pies,
Invisible strings cause my mind to rise.

Blurry snapshots of marvelous fun,
Chasing ideas like a startled bun.
Each tumble and twist, a blindfolded ride,
Fragments of nonsense I cannot hide.

Colors scatter in a nonsensical rush,
Thoughts collide in a playful hush.
Lost in the clutter of yarn and thread,
I tuck in laughter, and tuck in dread.

With each wobbly step, I trip and grin,
In the circus of thought, where delights begin.
Funny shapes flit through my head, dear,
In a patchwork of whimsy, I disappear.

www.ingramcontent.com/pod-product-compliance
Lightning Source LLC
Chambersburg PA
CBHW070313120526
44590CB00017B/2653